CANTATA
for a desert poet

CANTATA
for a desert poet

Sharon Lopez Mooney

New York

Thanks to the California Quarterly Poetry
Review, Visible Magazine, Sybil Journal, Unlikely
Stories, Kennings Literary Journal, The UNIverse
Journal, swifts & slows, and NewVerse News,
in which some of these poems first appeared.

Thanks also to Anton Shammas,
Palestinian writer, poet, and translator of Arabic,
Hebrew, and English, for his help in
the preparation of Salam Khalili's poems.

Cover painting by Salam Khalili

Arteidolia Press
arteidolia.com/arteidolia-press

First Edition
Library of Congress Control Number: 2023923847
ISBN 979-8-9889702-3-1

عهد ..

الى ابنتي «فلسطين»
الى ابني «نضال»
والى جميع أبناء شعبي

سـأحرقُ كلَّ أشعاري
إذا عجزتُ عن استيعابِ
تاريخي ومأساتي
نضالي وانتصاراتي
إذا لم تَرْسُم الأشعارُ
صورةَ وجهيَ الآتي..!

عبدالسلام

A Promise

To my daughter Falastine, to my son Nidal
and to all the children of my people

I will burn all my poems if I fail to
embrace my history and tragedy,
my struggles and my victories, if my poems do
not paint the picture of my emerging self!

Abdulsalam

Salam Khalili

PREFACE

Cantata for a Desert Poet commemorates a wish of Mohamed Abdulsalam Khalili, who was a Palestinian journalist, painter, poet, and peace activist before, during, and after the Six-Day War in 1967. In 1973, as a chief editor at Jerusalem's weekly newspaper *El Fajr*, he published an article with evidence that the war had been preplanned, prearranged, and agreed upon by Israel and Jordan. Because he did not first get permission to publish, he was taken as prisoner by Israel, tried, given a twenty-five-year sentence, and subsequently tortured for seven years. He was then put under house arrest for three years more before a small group of western journalists pressured Amnesty International to step in and fight for his freedom.

Subsequently, Salam was exiled from Palestine by Israel, and he and his family were then relocated to the United States by a concerned and generous sponsor. Twenty years after his arrest, the truth in his article came to light.

He spent the rest of his life engaged in California wherever he could be, working to encourage and support the development of an agreement between Palestine and Israel to find a compromise and share the land they all love in peace and equality. He welcomed into his home many young immigrant Arab men as well as others dispersed by the terrors in the Middle East. In his later years, he became a frequent speaker at Spirit Rock Meditation Center on forgiveness, building peace and cooperation, and other personal spiritual topics. He and Jack Kornfield became friends, and Buddhism offered him a practice of solace for his aching soul.

Salam and I met in California, where he settled and we became intimates. He continued to try to paint but was never able to regain his brush. He tried writing, but was never able to find his poet's way into written English although he remained a master Palestinian poet and a poetic storyteller in oral English. He asked me to tell his one man's story in my own original poetry for him. He laid his hope of sharing his truths in my hands, believing them the same struggles as so many affected by war. The storylines of these poems are inspired by stories he gifted to me, and I have considered it a sacred charge from this political and spiritual poet. Salam died in 2016 at the young age of 64 without he or his two adult children ever being allowed to return to their beloved Jerusalem. The struggle continues on many fronts.

This book is admiringly dedicated to
Salam Khalili.

HUMAN COLLATERAL
a lament

PREFACE

CHANCE ENCOUNTER

THE IN-BETWEEN

THE RETURNING

As part of Salam's imprisonment, more than 125 paintings and an immeasurable count of books, documents, and papers were incinerated by the authorities.

With each chapter heading is a section of the one poem written in his own hand from among the few papers secreted away by his family. Salam describes a Palestinian girl on a windy day, crying as she is walking to school. He saw the girl from the window of the police car the day he was arrested.

The poem is incomplete, ending abruptly on the last page, and it is clear that there are more stanzas, but those are missing. We have included these pages to give his poet's voice and artist's hand one more chance to be heard.

Sharon Lopez Mooney

Chance
encounter

حَتَّى عُيونِكِ الْحِلْوِين
بِالْحُزْنْ طَفْحَانِين
وْحَبَّاتْ لُولُو مْفَرْقَطَهْ عَالْخَدْ؟
شُو صَارْ حَتَّى تْمَرْمَغِ الْمَرْيُولْ
هَالْأَزْرَقِ الْمَبْلُولْ
وَانْقَطَعَتِ الشَّنْتِهْ؟
يِمْكِنْ تْزَحْلَقْتِي
ـ دَسْتُورْ ! ـ
فِي هَالطِّينْ
مِنْ كُتْرْ مَا كِنْتِي
عَمْ تُرْكْضِي ..
وِالْمَدْرَسِهْ بْعِيدِه؟

California – Alchemy of a life

Exiled from Jerusalem, his belongings stamped illegal, a few paintings saved in the downdraft as he fled, his poems became dust in the left behind. He never found his poet's voice on pieces of western paper, but found me, a northern California poet, who he caught in his web of magical storytelling. We, he and I, became one heart in many achingly delicate, late night shadows of his home in a warehouse's echo — his refuge hidden off a dim industrial side-street of an urban landscape.

He composed a symphony of tales that had not been erased, etudes of memory that caressed his heart each rising sun, and were extinguished again each night by the scars of those who could still reach across the decades. This Desert Poet whispered stories so I could be his pen, the song he would never sing, and share his journey in the sunshine and neon city where finally he release into death.

Our first evening

"I really like brass washers" he says putting the dirty metal
screw through the hole of his shiny new invention
he's always inventing a new machine to exercise his creativity
words pass in spirals slipping and sliding through hidden feelings
that circle but sometimes I see them at the edges of his eyes laughing
I am sure he can sense my hunger although I have learned to be quiet

I say provocative lines he answers quick easy and I think he knows
we are nimble in our dance yet we trip and fall entangled
in words and meanings and messages unstated and full of the poetry
he pours out into the room drawing images and stories ripe with longing
thick with undercurrents piled up next to the six brass washers
I pick them up and slide them around in the smooth of my palm
we keep finding each other eye to eye with silent messages
the other cannot hear in this crowded noisy room filled with silence

I long to hear him pour out words that can reveal what he wants
from me and why I am here, but I don't even think to ask because
we have already learned to read the silent signals that so
voluptuously slide between us, our words like washers on the table
scatter and our forming thoughts dissolve in the flurry of clatter
and people coming into the pregnant room it is time to stop. He
carries our attraction to his private treasure box I sweep our left over
disarranged words into my pockets so I can go over them again and
again later alone. Someone reaches out turns off the light

Soul of his people

He opens the soul of his people to me
reliving his time on the sultry rooftops
of his cherished Jerusalem.
I smell lamb and spices, the sweat of hard labor,
the exuberance in children stealing giggles
safely behind garden gates.

In his cluttered workshop in this foreign country
he paints landscapes of Jerusalem on the floor
where he teaches me to rest
as we become desert meeting sky
lying on concrete broken into melodic memories.
Music makes love to us as I watch him work.
  I've become keeper of his soul
  his homeland
  his treasured secrets.

His humming fuses us into one moment
refracted dark, moist, fecund bittersweet past
where he becomes the words he weaves
composing life with images that run through
us like the wild war horses he saw
crossing hot sand at dusk.

Gliding back and forth
between harsh brilliant days of the Sinai Desert
and cool silence of Northern California drizzle
he sketches the casualties of war, the cries
of innocence lost in the hearts of children
along my horizon.

I've been given his voice, his awful truths,
and asked to give birth to this requiem.

Oh, Children of War!

I want to read something to you. I will translate. Salam laid the newspaper clipping on the desk. He read the list of boys, none over twelve, shot by soldiers in the West Bank of Palestine, twelve in all in twenty months of the "Intifada". He painfully read their names, ages, how they died. In the middle of the list was Ahmad, he the youngest, six.

Wafa and I sat still as photographs while Salam translated the small article about this youngest victim, his fingers slowly moving across the lines of type, right to left, as though they were trying to soothe the pain. He continues loosely translating...*the very day Ahmad died, his mother gave birth to a new son and they named the baby after him.* Salam read how she would not lay the baby down.

Since Ahmad was four, old enough to be out in the hard alone, he carried a stone in his closed fist or pocket, never without a stone, even inside the house, always a stone. Last year on vacation, his parents turned to find him throwing stones at a passing police car and rushed to tell him the police in Egypt were friendly, he was safe, no need for stones. But even then he kept a small stone tucked in his little clenched fingers because in his little life shooting and death were constant, were heard on all sides every day, because being wounded and dying happened to his uncle, his neighbors, his friends.

That morning, now that he was six, his father had sent Ahmad to the store to buy cigarettes. As he came out of the shop, bigger boys on the roof above him were hurling stones at the patrolling Israeli soldiers. The soldiers splayed the street and buildings with rubber bullets and Ahmad was shot in the head and killed.

Earlier Ahmad had made a game to play with his father. He would run into the house and say, *Baba, Baba, Ahmad has been shot, Ahmad has been shot!* His father would fall to the floor pretending to cry and wail for his son. The six year old boy would spring out, throwing himself on his father gleefully and cry, *No, no I am alive! Ahmad is alive!* And they would dance and celebrate.

Salam looked up from the paper and saw Wafa with his face tipped downward, fidgeting with his watch. He lifted his head and spoke in Arabic.

Go then! Go in the other room and pray, it is fine. Salam returned to the news clipping.

Is it really prayer time, Salam? I wiped my eyes as I watched Wafa bow into his prayer through the doorway. *Doesn't it ever make you cry?*

Not much anymore. One cries for so many deaths, so many years, so many children the sorrow is so deep that the tears grow far away. In the late afternoon silence, over and over he caressed the names with his fingers, Ayman 11 years, Hani 12 years, Ahmad 6 years old...

A life of walls

He was a curious child to them,
their passionate dreamer
small boy poet, their son,
hours alone, stubby pencil to scrap of paper
hiding his hunger in words,
his heart so delicate,
there was no safe place
in the strange jordanland of escape,
so he hid his poems in sand walls.

When he came of age, he returned
to the heart of his country's history,
burying his soul in a deep grave
alongside those of his peoples, laid down
on that embrace of land, exposed war secrets
in daily print news, promised his life
to regain the peoples' freedom, allowing fire
to consume his years in the agony
of prison walls built for lies and torture.

In the dark of pain and bars
held in place by bloody bricks of loss
one remembers promises like that,
news comrades learned of his trial by conflagration,
fought for his freedom to only beget
his sequestered living behind invisible walls
surrounding his home, converting it
to a political territory, blocking his friends,
his voice, trying to destroy their dream.

Finally, in the crux of expulsion from his motherland,
sponsors chose a distant new home for him
and his children, into an unfamiliar life
of abundance with more invisible barriers he did not
make, with no passage back to his desert love,
with her soiled lands strewn with the victor's
dirty tricks, where they burned his poems
shredded his paintings.

Exhausted, he drew in breath
in this new city offering freedom
and readied himself to build again,
against his intuition of what really lay ahead
he unfurled their dreams into new potential futures
for them all who would never see home.
And the price this time also was great,
they found new unspoken barriers, hidden deceits,
but this time to restrain their souls.

Gift from Father

He rolled over on the single bed turning his face away from me. His voice was deep with fatigue, tone brooding as he reached for another memory.

I was traveling my way back from the newspaper office. The street was hushed, radiated heat. In one explosive moment I knew I had been shot, the searing came long before I heard the shot. Lying as still as possible, I listened. Nothing. Where were the others? Could I stand up? I rolled over twice, slowly, the pain so intense it shot down my legs cramping them. Swallowing my scream and with great effort I edged my way up against the building. Was I safe? Yes. I was not visible from the street, there was no movement anywhere. But it was late afternoon, there would be many hours before the safety of dark.

Slowly, hesitatingly, I looked down to the pain in my abdomen, immediately slamming my eyes shut. *Shit!* My mind tripped over itself. Shaking beyond control, I opened my eyes and again began the cautious descent to my midsection. I could not believe what I was seeing. It appeared my stomach was missing, just an empty hole of blood. If I made noise vomiting, the soldiers would find me, so I held my breath, closed my eyes, pressed my head against the hot wall swallowing revulsion and waited.

I knew I was dying. There was no way I could get up, no way to make any sound for help, no way to live without a stomach. I will die. Just then there was a confusion of soldiers and even my thoughts froze.

Nothing to do. I made myself as small as possible. How does one prepare to die? Fear cramped my mind. Pushing through, I looked down to my wound again, but noticed a spot of blood on the knee of the pants my father had given me. I had taken such great care to only wear them on special occasions. And now, blood! A stain of blood...if it dried, it would never come out. I was frantic. What could I do?

I looked around for something, a rag, a scrap, when I saw my shirt tail hanging out. With all my strength and with slow deliberate moves I tore off a piece of cloth, raised it to my mouth ignoring the fire racing through my body. I slowly pushed the pain out of my way, wet the blue cotton with saliva and reached down to the bloody spot.

Straining every nerve and muscle, I worked with tense focus, before it dried. It was as though I moved outside my body to some safe ground where I could work wetting the cloth, rubbing, rewetting, rubbing in slow motion. I had to get it out. If it dried, if it dried there would be no hope at all. I fought against the difficulty of making enough saliva from my dried lips. With total focus I rubbed and spit and rubbed and gradually a small tip of the spot began to lighten. I was filled with hope, I could save the pants! I continued, concentrating like a doctor saving lives.

Off to the side there was a whisper. *Here he is! He's been hit! Come help me get him out of here! Salam, it's alright now, forget the pants. Salam! Salam forget the damn pants!*

The poet's memories of war wear him down

He stands isolated
in a dancehall packed with laughing strangers
and, like last time, like all the times,
holds himself tight against what might
happen, but never does, never shows its face.

Drums beat the earth under him
brass horns pulse against his chest
her body is swaying fluid, a river
of music pumps thoughtless pleasure through him,
she is the liquid hot forgetting
of vodka he sweats out soaking his clothes
as he drinks her in deeply.

But in the vacuum between songs
he remembers the children, *God! what
has been done to the children!*
It lacerates his breast, sears his brain,
old bombs explode, ripping his guts
there is nowhere to go, nowhere.

Nowhere in the press of panting bodies
to sop up the memories of suffering,
put pressure against the bleeding, he
reaches for her, the strand of life he tangles into,
his hand lands on the close shore
of her cool running river, she stops,
has seen the flash
of fire rockets in his eyes.

They are stranded, lost together for
an endless moment, silent, suspended,
music returns in soothing waves,
singing the moon. He dives into her
pleasure of mindless movement,
collateral cries and moans of war float into silence
again he is free once more for another interlude.

Prisoner of war at home

Death has sucked on him and spit him out
from beyond dream almost to forever,
but some insistence yanks him back
back into horror and broken teeth.

> *Make my heart beat faster, make it catch up!*

Pressing his chest, he massages,
life is running out ahead dragging
him a frayed rope-end of leash,
he waits out the long slow stretch of time.

Now at home, still those years succeed
in breaking him (their goal all along),
they haunt his effort to rebuild, and still
derail his children's futures.

> *Why, still, do I have to live in this body bag of flesh*
> *the only thing they left me ....*

Official records, lists of documented facts,
hours of interviews — he spoke until his voice
broke in his heart — still it changed nothing,
disturbing secrets drown his voice into silence.

With each boot blow to his ribs, each
metal rod's smash on his back, hate
broke him into pieces that rattle
inaudibly with his tiniest step.

> Why can I only live in this debris of broken ribs,
> only pretend to, not remembering
> the stink of my body on that cell floor,
> remember death's rancid taste in my saliva?

Running his hands over hair on his legs
he makes it into smooth, minute lines
remembering tiny hairline cracks
on the walls of the cell, his only shelter.

Too weak to put pressure where
he felt a leak of warm blood,
he moved just outside himself again
where it was safe and blank.

Tonight he lies on his bed
in the empty echo of his homemade cell
in the makeshift home, watching headlights
arc across the walls of his room.

> There must be some reason
> why I should want to be alive
> there must be some reason,
> there must be some ...

The
in-between

لَو كَانْ فِي إِيدِي

أَعْمِلْ جَنَاحْ وُ طِيرْ

تَا وَصَّلِكْ بَكِّيرْ

تَا مَسِّح الدَّمْعَهْ عَن جْفُونِكْ

أَللَّهْ مَعِكْ يَا شَاطْرَهْ

يْصُونِكْ ..

لٰكِنْ

ـ يَ حَسْرَهْ ـ

سَاعْدِي مَغْلُولْ

وِقْيُودْ فِي رِجْلَيَّ

وِ بْشَكْلْ مُشْ مَعْقُولْ مُشْ مَعْقُولْ

Where our story changes

In white tight shorts and black tee shirt
he stretches over the pool table, joking
with his son's young friends about
a fancy shot he bets twenty dollars on.
Hot afternoon sun beats heat waves through
double open doors of the warehouse
I smelled fear earlier when I walked
into the shade of the high ceilinged room
watched the hair on my arms raise, sensing
what we dreaded most was about to happen.

He feeds me melted chocolate ice cream on bread
my car gets washed, he watches me slyly
shows me how to buff out scratches
before he beats another young man in a lazy game.
These young middle-eastern men keep his
memories close but out of mind like the other
apostles around the supper table, I wait
unsure, and know there is brooding danger here
waiting for someone else to act.

His young son's embarrassed body teaches me
to lambada, but he is awkward
unsure of how to hold one of his father's lovers,
his daughter goes home, someone else gets binoculars
to watch the new prostitute working the corner,
they finally guess it, she's a cop.

He taps me playfully between shots, pool cue
never laid down, always another young man
anxious to try beating *The Father.*

Waiting presses on me like stifling air
of a steam room, I want to escape but
cannot raise my voice to say goodbye, a car stops
across the street, they make a deal
while video cameras catch his face, proof!
He's arrested, friends from a business next door
come to talk over the sting, wave to the cops
known from this often repeated neighborhood drama.

Spicy chicken wings make him fan his lips
      I must have at least one, he moans,
burgers, tabouli, chocolate birthday cake, hummus ...
he introduces his young nephew from Palestine, we all
know he will not stay so innocent in America.

As I ready to leave, he pulls me
to him with eyes of sadness and fear, whispers
      I cannot go on this way, torn
      between her and you.
The warehouse sighs, I cannot even nod,
he is scared by my blankness
squeezes my hand as I try to leave, sighs,

She helped bring us here, makes sure
there is money, the other women don't count
there is no other way for us in this crazy country.

I try to leave,
he will not let me go, tears threaten
clog his voice, it cracks
    but I will try
    I want you here
I try again to leave, whisper
    I must leave
    I must, I am late
    you cannot have it both ways
my feet don't move.

You trying to make home

Pulling into the parking lot, I see through open double
metal doors into a small warehouse, a man making home

with bright red paintings, filtered memories and retold stories
decorating the cold concrete walls and curious machines,

crazy inventions with cobalt blue wires and sunshine colors
poke out from surprising spots, all fashioning seductive comfort

with heart open and filled with belief in healing
you pause and raise your eyes to the bright light

that lazes through a lone high window, you reach out
caress it with a gentle hand as though massaging its hope

you a battered man making new life, drawing possibilities
for your son and your daughter, daring to dream

a different promise for them, built with your pain
sculpted by your courage, you are a man building

their futures with your own practice of peace, you a poet
telling stories of the past, an artist painting images of the new

building blocks for fresh dreams, you tremble as if it were cold,
but continue drawing a different world for all the children

still knowing it will not be

Father from Jerusalem

The father's daughter falls from him
into a risky, borrowed country
as tears from his aching eyes
she steals away one iota at a time
he's tried drawing her back
but she slips down crevices of sorrow in his
face, splashing onto the workshop floor.

He moves through the old warehouse
where his son shoots from his fingertips
when he lights a cigarette, inhales smoke
breathing his elusive son back
but can only hold him
until he must exhale again
into the chill of the foreign evening.

On Tuesday the father is frantic
with their seeping from him
so, he carves tables, builds sumptuous chairs
paints them fire and sunshine, furnishing a home
with hope, desperate to lure them to stay
in their safety nest, but no one returns,
only the mice make home with him.

Friday, exhausted on the tomb cold floor
the father lies against bright colored images
of mosques and houses made of Jerusalem stone,
memories burnt into his heart of forbidden return
are sketched onto the cement where he waits
cradling himself against nightmares of his children
pouring from him into violent red pools

Sunday the heat makes everything trickle away,
he cannot find safety for them in this camouflaged
country of mistrust and illusions so stands in the doorway
facing harsh sunlight, his back to the dark threatening
with its shadow shifting world lying in wait,
he is suspended in this uncomfortable
waiting where he cannot act for his own sake.

He will make the next leg in this life journey
for his eyes where his daughter lives,
for his hands where his son plans the future,
he will build bridges to ease his daughter's passage,
will slow his son's too rapid firing into manhood,
they are barred from returning home, held
in a country that fits like another's discarded clothes.

He will methodically make possible their safe futures
with great cost to his heart.

His heart cries as he tries to paint his way home

He is frozen here, painting a chaos of color,
red burns into fire recoloring the strength
of his patron's will, she hopes to inspire him
her polished pewter shoulders the reason he is still alive.

He, a Jerusalem firebrand poet, is drowning in help
of wealthy western sponsors, their passions fueled his flight,
they chose this unbroken country of liberty and freedom
recklessly wasted in this youngster of a nation,

he lays thick warrior red over his canvas,
but their adulation spreads as stain in all directions,
falsely ennobling his endless journey
from his beloved city, his Jerusalem.

Maybe, maybe, when the paint is dry,
the aching will release him and his children,
to return to plant their bare feet on the land
of their birth, his mother and lover, their Jerusalem.

Maybe finally, this palette of a new neon life,
gifted him in spite of his constant yearning to go back,
will offer passage home to the land of their blood,
but their hope pushes against forbidden return.

Little bird from the desert

He watched through a barbed wired cut-away window past the
patrolled prison into morning desert. A guard turned staring. *We
are nowhere*, Salam mused, hungering for release in his cell-
bound aloneness. Big and tough, dark and mean, a war prison
shelters no gentleness.

On a day after an especially vicious torture session in '69, sunny
and hot, a tiny trumpeter finch fell from a hidden nest, shivering
and fragile, onto the outside ledge of his suggestion of a window.
He could not reach the little bird so watched for what might have
been hours as it slowly inched its way through the tiny barbed
wire holes searching, into his reach.

Cradling the barely breathing bundle, Salam tucked it inside his
shirt for warmth as he built a nest in the corner of his sleeping
pile on the scarred cement floor. Each day he saved parts of the
lukewarm meal slid in along the cool floor, to feed drop by drop,
fathering the fledgeling. Against odds, it slowly grew strong
enough to practice flying in the tiny cell, and finally, one empty
evening, it took off through the bars, down the ominous hall, a
flit of life past guards and prisoners who peered and laughed at
the surprise, through unfriendly steel bars.

He made his little flight of hope back and forth, past dreary cells
and guards on post, for many days, always returning to Salam,
his family. He became known as *Salam's little bird*. In less time
than any of them wanted, *little bird* came into his small, mature
self, hungering for something missing and squeezed back out
through the wire mesh window into the free.

In the days after *little bird's escape*, the nasty hall guard and the Russian immigrant guard, seemed to soften toward Salam, even acting without malice. Since *little bird's* leaving, there seemed to be a new grief haunting their prison section affecting prisoners and guards alike.

Salam watched as joy flew away in an instant. He stood at the window until dark waiting for *little bird* to return home. He stood at the tiny window every day with a diminishing sliver of hope, watching the horizon. But then he saw. He saw in the corner of the prison yard, *little bird* searching the empty dirt. His hope began to awaken, and he started leaving bits of food on the ledge, tempting, calling *little bird* home. One chilled dawn, he noticed the patrolling guard discretely dropping bits of food along the edge of the walls. *Little bird* began to come each early morning.

A few days later, Salam heard a strange rushing noise drawing toward his cell. He stepped to the bars and saw the yard guard frantically stop at his cell with tears. In desperate sobs, he whispered, *Salam you must bring him back! He's hurt, fix him!* But even the gentle touch of familial hands could not bring back life.

They stood stark and unmoving on each side of the bars, eyes caressing *little bird* lying quiet in Salam's hands. Once his composure was back, the guard opened the door, stepped into the cell, explaining in hushed tones that he was on patrol, eyes busy, when he stepped on something soft. He stooped, recognizing *little bird*, tenderly picked him up to find no life, a state he knew too well in wartime.

He looked Salam in the eye, slowly stepped closer, surprising him, and begged quietly, *Please forgive me for killing little bird. I did not know he was there, I was busy watching...* with breaking voice his face lowered to hide tears burning his heart. He told Salam how much he had come to love *little bird*.

Once again, they hesitated in bleak silence. *Of course, I forgive you,* Salam softly consoled. The guard reached, putting his arms around Salam where they held each other inside a secret they now shared and feared would be discovered. Waiting together in a gentle heartbeat of loss, they then stepped back to resume their established enemy roles.

Over time the forgiven guard and Salam became secret friends sharing stories of families and youthful adventures in bits and snippets. Salam drew a portrait on a scape of paper of the guard with his family from a picture his new friend snuck to him through the wired window. Military police had confiscated and burned over a hundred of his paintings before they could be sent to family when he was arrested. But the guard snuck his family portrait out after work, and later cleverly smuggled twenty other oil paintings into the care of Salam's family before they could be incinerated according to rules.

On an angry day, Salam was called to the warden's office. As he was shoved into the room, the warden noticed him glancing toward one of his paintings sloppily hung on the ash colored wall, alone, centered as though spotlighted, *the portrait of a lion behind bars.* After the meeting of vicious warnings and life endangering threats, the warden dismissed him with a smirk saying, *You see, even if you were lions, we can still put you behind bars.*

Moving toward the door, Salam stopped, with his back to the warden, stood for a frozen moment, and after a deep inhale continued walking, turning his head over his shoulder, looked at the painting and said, *Oh no, on the contrary, Warden, even if you put us behind bars we are still lions.*

Love triangle with Jerusalem

You paint dreams
feelings
quiet despair
in small wordstrokes
with insistent hunger
for the desert still gnawing on you

You sit across, naked on the couch,
smoking the way men in war do,
this is lovemaking talking this way
several arm lengths apart,
my breast fills with sweet longing
my toes wiggle

Sensing the shape of this inevitability
you inhale tears through
the *Kool's* filter, exhale
only smoke,
there is nothing you can do,
with me you could catch fire

Even in this foggy city
you are a desert dweller,
believe I live in flames where you
fear you would lose yourself,
and yet, you return,
extinguish your cigarette,
lay down, inhaling me

I caress the sharp line
of your jaw as you turn your face
to her, your desert, your Jerusalem, so close
nothing can lie between you,
you begin painting again
with words on my body

The
returning

عِيني عَم تْنَاضِلْ
حَتَّى تْبُوس الضَّيّ
هَالْمِنْعِكِسْ مِنْ دَمعِكِ الْهَاطِلْ
زَيّ الْجَوَاهِرْ عَا صِدرْ مَرْمَرْ

سْنِتِينْ .. أَوْ أَكْتَرْ ..
تَحتِ اللأَرِضْ مَحْبُوسْ
في الْعِتْمِه
والشَّمْسْ مَا مَرّتْ عَلَى جِبِيني
وَرَغْمِ الضّرِبْ وِالْجُوعْ وِالنّقْمِه
مَا دَمَّعَتْ عِيني !

A Scent of Green

Were you afraid? His answer was smooth and even like water spilling over a glass table. *No, I was not. It was a different world, a different time. I floated in a sea somewhere. I can remember now, she was beautiful, soft and smelled like trees. She was a neighbor and when I was three, her husband was gone for long periods in the conflicts. She had no children and was very lonely.*

She used to borrow me from my mother at night. My mother was very young with several children and grateful to her. The woman would read me stories and at bedtime, she would wash me as one does a child, caress me, kiss my hands and belly and little three year old penis and it would get hard. I make no judgment about it.

There were many things to fear, but not at home, not her. Afraid of silencing him, I drew my words up from sorrow cautiously, making them calm and quiet. *What if that happened to a little girl, to your daughter? Would you think differently?*

He paused, head turned as though listening to the night outside, lifted the curtain to see the empty street. *Once when my son was little, the babysitter did that to him, well, some things happened, and when I found out, I was angry! I could probably have killed her right there.*

But that kind of rage accomplishes nothing. I did not turn her in, you did not turn anyone in to the authoritiesß. I talked to her a long time trying to make her see her wrong, then banished her from our lives.

He ran his finger over the cool windowsill next to the bed, and then across the outline of my body lying face away from him, dark profile against the dim lamplight. *But I do not make judgment about what happened with me. I do not view it as right or wrong. Oh, I know now, it should not have happened.*

It should happen to no child, ever. And still, I can remember the smoothness of her skin, the scent of green of her bed as I fell asleep. There is some mysterious pleasure in the memory.

He sat up slowly, pulling the pillow behind him, leaned against the wall gazing into the shadowy room, seeing nothing, silence as companion. *Then from the time I was about eight, I was very sexual with girls who were older than me. These hands you said the other night were 'so beautiful?'*

He looked at his hand relaxed on my body, *I was born with them, you know, I can take no credit for them. Sometimes I laugh at them, sometimes I cry. How they long to touch women. No, I have no judgment about what happened with her.*

Father, was the price too high?

History accosts him with the nothing
of childhood he could have done differently,
caught in a web of conniving for money,
clever methods for work, and he learned,
got smarter as he aged, sold his knowledge, his charm,
became a word and brushstroke warrior defiant for freedom
bold for his people, his children,
against those who stole their land their hopes.

Now afar, he craves Jerusalem, sensuous city seized
she bled through his veins, bound him to her
his home where he is not allowed to return,
punishment for refusing to be silent,
       A cost too great?
Skeleton bones rattle with every step he takes
as he talks over their business with his son, he feels
the ache of those years when war against war, its demand,
       its seduction, took from him a grave toll,
       his son, a daughter, his family.

He burns with unanswerable questions
could he have done it differently? Did he do it again,
sell himself to flight, to safety, to promised freedom?
       Did I, father?
In 'this land of the free, home of the brave' where he still craves
freedom, the past sears his memory into ash, blows it
across fecund black earth, cool, quiet, safe,

Am I doing it, father? Trading
my promise for their freedom?
is the price once more, too great?
invisible under the public mask he wears, the scars
throb faithfully reminding history is what he made,
and history married him to the destiny of his people
where each vow could have been a thousand others.
He lays in lost midnights, awake, feeling the pulse
of the past pounding in his body
praying the price this time is not his soul.

Dying from a different kind of arid

He leans against winter shadows with such great sorrow,
longing to conjure peace, as a magician might drink
sacred water before a birth. Cupping a cigarette like men
in war do, he inhales a California city's back streets,
exhales his fear, he can feel his Jerusalem dying, she needs him.
But he cannot go back as he begins to embrace his own dying.
He whispers his hope that his loss of belonging has not burned
right through him scaling his children's futures.
Outside an occasional car passes in the rain
sounds of wet whipping on the street.

He flips the remote shutting the tv off,
our silence bangs against the heater, he draws
the blinds partly closed, says he longs to bring
Jerusalem here, heart of his, held captive when
they banished him, forbade return. But now
the desert warrior is dying. His heels still stick out
bare from shoes worn as a desert man does
no socks in winter, backs forced flat,
he makes sandals of every shore he wears
hoping still maybe he can one day return.

He is tumbling within shifting sands changing
his entire world. He is glad I do not believe his fear
remembering he asked me to be his faith while he is lost
in eternally damnable dark. Jerusalem was more than home
she was his lover, his self, everything he did, every battle
he waged, every poem he wrote was for her, his beloved.
His soul still nests in the crotch of that sacred city,
no longer able to return home, he sits back and cries.
A siren grows louder, screams past the windows
fades into fog. At three a.m. the concrete city outside is quiet.

None of us quite let him go

Standing outside the warehouse door
of his business and mock home, with an open
invisible door, I hesitate to walk through into dark.
He has been sweeping the floor with colorful
ideas for paintings, they lie half finished,
scuffed and darkened by shoes of so many friends,
family and even a few footprints from me
USA born woman enraptured by him.
>   *Oh, love, you have come. I've*
>   *been waiting. It's been too long. Come,*
>   *please come. Do you want some*
>   *yogurt cheese? I just finished it.*

>   *No, Salam, nothing, just to visit with you.*

>   *Come, I'm going to lay down, come.*

He moves, a mature man in a ravaged man's body,
bends, twisting cautiously to roll onto his slightly
made bed. He peeks out to where he makes business
and art and inventions, all tossed, never completed
a snapshot of his life.
>   *Habibi, sit here,* he calls with his beautiful hands,
>   *sit near me, so we can talk. No, lay here with me?*
>   *I miss your warmth, your woman's body.*

>   *Oh, it's such a little bed, and I can't stay long ....*

He looks nearly how he did ten years ago, an almost aching
beauty still radiates from his eyes, musical tones still play on his lips,
but oh, his energy has faded, barely a whispered force
  My pants pockets still brim with stories
  I try to paint them, but no, because still,
  only you are my words.

We smile and talk of whats and thens, chuckle about who
and whens, talking as easy as it ever was. I can see
his hands want to touch me, but he lays quiet
facing me with a moan of longing and sadness.
Ten years has built a polite wall neither of us tries to climb.
  Tell me about your poems, you are still writing?
  I hope so! My stories are yours now. Tell me,
  please, come closer. Is the bird story written?

I describe the obstacles to catching and giving poetics
to the drama of his life, and am embarrassed I cannot yet
hand him a beautiful volume. He smiles and turns over,
grunts just enough to let me know he needs a massage,
the old familiar love exchange. I cannot help him
this afternoon, laying my hands on him ignites
a fire I am not ready to burn again.

I begin to mutter the lines one says to leave a place
that threatens in the most seductive, essential ways.
He turns, looks at me, *OK,* he whispers. I say I will come
back sometime, it won't be two years again.

> *It is fine. Anyway, I am done, I will leave soon.*

> *No, Salam....Nooo....so many love you*

> *Oh yes, I know you know dying is safe.*
> *Sometime soon this broken body will no longer belong here*
> *it has endured much and has completed all its work,*
> *my children have been consumed by living,*
> *no longer only mine. My flight left long ago. I am ready.*
> *There's nothing more to be done.*

Instinctively I reach for him across fecund, open space.
He holds his gaze on me, does not move, says nothing more,
simply shrugs in his easy familiar way. Smiling our hands touch, hold for
a few short minutes and then fall apart. I inhale, get up, walk away
feeling the caress of his eyes loving me this last time,
out through the invisible door, from darkness into the alone
of a brilliant day in a small ugly parking lot.